African American

True Heroes of the Old West

By Jeffrey B. Fuerst

Celebration Press
Pearson Learning Group

Contents

Real Cowboys

You may have seen old movies or heard old songs about brave cowboys in the Old West who do great deeds and then ride off into the sunset. From these stories you might think there were no African American cowboys— but you would be wrong. There were many outstanding African American cowboys who used their skills to make important contributions to the development of the West.

Two African American cowboys are among this crew of ranch hands.

Chances are you have never read any books or watched any old movies about the following cowboys.

Bose Ikard He was an expert **trailblazer**, who helped establish the famous Goodnight-Loving Trail. This was one of a handful of routes cowboys used to drive millions of cattle from Texas to western territories like Colorado.

Bass Reeves In his 32 years as a U.S. deputy marshal in Indian Territory, few criminals escaped him. His knowledge of Native American languages helped him communicate with people who lived in the Territory, which is now part of Oklahoma. To catch outlaws, the clever Reeves disguised himself as a trail rider, drifter, or outlaw.

U.S. Marshal, Bass Reeves

James Arthur Walker

Also known as "One Horse Charlie," he was a master at rope tricks and was also a brilliant rider. You may have seen cowboy movie stunt riders do a trick some say he invented—riding a horse at full speed and then jumping to the ground and hopping back on while the horse is running.

Extraordinary cowboy James Arthur Walker

Bronco Sam Here was a truly wild Old West character. For the fun of it, he once rode a snorting steer down the main street of Cheyenne, Wyoming. When the steer saw itself in a shop window, it thought it was seeing another steer. So it charged—right into the window!

Why were there so few books, movies, or TV shows about these real Old West cowboys? One reason is that they were African Americans. In the past, book publishers and movie companies didn't produce many stories about African American characters.

Another reason is that most stories about cowboys are "tall tales" told to entertain. Some are based on true events and real people. However, in their telling, the truth was stretched. Real cowboys often became fictional characters.

Made-up stories about cowboys "cleaning up the West" are more exciting than what actually happened. A cowboy's job was really to tend cattle along millions of acres of wide-open public lands stretching from Texas to Montana.

About 5,000 of the 30,000 cowboys who rode the range in the 1870s and 1880s were African American.

Although a cowboy's life could be exciting, it was often lonesome. Most Old West cowboys slept under the stars for months at a time and got to town only once or twice a year.

However, these hard-working men helped build the nation's cattle industry. Also, by moving cattle long distances to the nearest railroad town, they helped open the way for our country's westward expansion. About 5,000 of these cowboys—one out of six—were African Americans.

Up From Slavery

Before the Civil War (1861–1865), Texas allowed slavery. Many slaves worked on cattle ranches and learned valuable skills from *vaqueros* (Mexican cowboys) who lived in Texas and from other cowboys on the ranch. They tamed wild horses. They **lassoed** the wild cattle that roamed free on the range. They chased after, wrestled with, and **branded** calves.

By the end of the Civil War, the long-horned wild cattle that lived in southern Texas had multiplied greatly and were free for the taking. But in sparsely populated Texas, cows and steers were worth only a few dollars each. If the cattle could somehow be transported east, where people paid high prices for beef, they could be sold for a huge profit.

Getting their cattle to market, however, was a big problem for ranchers. In those days there weren't any trucks or highways! The closest railroads were hundreds of miles to

Cowboys were skilled at roping calves.

the north in booming frontier towns like Abilene, Kansas. The only way to get cattle to these towns for shipping east was to herd them across the prairie.

Many former Texas slaves had the special skills ranchers needed to round up wild cattle and bring them to market. Other freed African Americans headed west where they also hoped to begin new lives as cowboys.

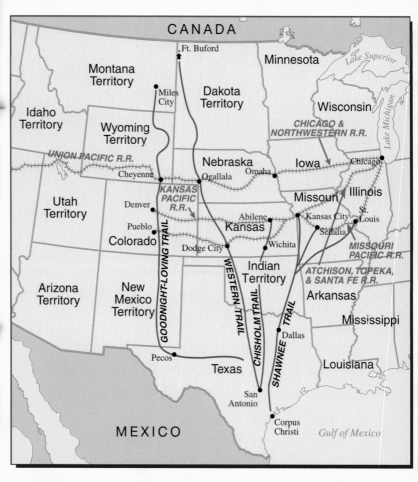

Cowboys drove cattle to railroad yards and to ranches farther north along several main routes.

Cattle Trails of the Old West

At first, cowboys and cattle trod dusty old trading routes and Native American trails. Problems soon arose from thieves as well as from farmers who tried to keep the cattle from crossing their land. As a result the cowboys blazed new trails from Texas to the stockyards and railroads in Kansas and Colorado. The popular Chisholm Trail offered good grazing and watering holes along the way.

Some routes continued on farther north. Pioneering cattle ranchers settled in the wilderness of Wyoming, Montana, and the Dakotas. Many African Americans moved to these new territories, too. They grabbed opportunity, found hope for a better life, and established farms and communities.

Life on the Trail

Herding cattle was a rough, dusty job.

On a typical cattle drive, about 10 or 12 cowboys handled a few thousand cattle. About two of these cowboys were African Americans. The cowboys traveled between 10 and 20 miles a day. Drives usually took place in the spring and summer and lasted about two to three months, sometimes longer.

Leading the way was the trail boss. He hired the crew and was responsible for delivering the cattle.

The trail boss usually rode ahead of the herd, scouting out water, **grazing** land, and possible trouble, such as cattle thieves. In addition, the trail boss picked the daily rest stops. He earned about $100 a month, high wages at that time.

The other cowboys earned between $25 and $45 a month, regardless of their color or race. This was unusual in the late 1800s, when most African Americans were denied equal opportunities. Although they rarely became trail bosses, African Americans held many of the other important positions, including point riders, swing riders, and flank riders.

The two most experienced cowboys were usually point riders. They rode at the head of the herd, set the pace, and led the cattle in the right direction. Behind them two swing riders and then two flank riders rode alongside the herd to keep cattle from straying.

Two drag riders followed behind the herd and made sure all animals kept up. Riding drag was considered the worst job. These cowboys "ate" the dust kicked up by cattle all day long.

A cattle-driving outfit might have 50 or more horses, which the **wrangler** cared for. He made sure each cowboy had a fresh mount twice a day. This job was often handled by a teenager.

The cook drove the all-important **chuck wagon**. This was a combination kitchen and supply shed on wheels. The cook was frequently African American and was often paid more than all the other cowboys—except the trail boss.

Like the trail boss, the cook rode ahead of the cattle and often was the first one to spot danger, such as wolves or **quicksand**. He also set up camp, cooked three meals a day, and tended to the cowboys' needs, as the crew's unofficial doctor and dentist. The cook was often a former cowboy, now too old (over 30!) to handle the physically hard task of riding a horse 10 to 14 hours a day.

Breakfast for the cowboys was served at dawn. It usually consisted of salt pork or bacon, hard sourdough biscuits, and dried fruit.

The second meal of the day was dinner. It was served around midday.

Supper was served at night after camp was made. Cowboys usually ate beef for supper. Sometimes steak would be served. At other times the main course was stew or beef tongues, hearts, and livers.

Along with meals, the cook often served wisdom and wisecracks to the young cowpokes.

Just surviving a long, tiring day in the saddle could be difficult. Cowboys risked danger at every bend in the trail. They might disturb a nest of snakes. Severe lightning and hailstorms were also common.

One of the many rivers they needed to cross could be running fast, swollen from spring rains. If it was deep, the cattle might have to swim. Cowboys on their horses as well as cattle might be swept away.

Crossing rivers could be dangerous for the cowboys as well as the cattle.

Sometimes to pass safely through Indian Territory, the trail boss needed to bargain and pay a fee—or suffer the consequences of attacks or stealing of cattle.

Most cowboys' biggest fear was of a **stampede**, a sudden running away of cattle. Longhorn cattle scared easily. The bang of a tin cup or the scrape of a match could set these animals running, as a group. Cowboys could be trampled and killed.

Only through teamwork could cowboys survive stampedes. They galloped on horses to the head of the herd and tried to turn the leaders around by yelling and firing pistols. Cowboys had to stick together; there was no time for quarrels on the trail.

A night's sleep for a cowboy was never more than six hours. At night they took turns watching over the herd. To keep their cattle calm, the cowboys would hum or sing lullabies and other songs. The sound of a human voice seemed to have a quieting effect on the cattle.

Cowboys at D
In th

This postcard shows cowboys eating dinner
after a day of rounding up horses.

Cowboys sang to each other, too, for
entertainment. On a long, lonely cattle drive,
a cowboy's co-workers were his friends and
family. They relied on one another for such
simple tasks as getting a haircut. They also
nursed one another when sick or injured.

Round up.

As members of a tight-knit group who depended on one another for daily survival, cowboys couldn't afford to treat some members differently. As long as a cowboy did his job, it usually didn't matter if his skin was white, black, red, or brown. African Americans working as cowboys were usually offered more equality than those in almost any other job in the country. Their wages were equal to those of white cowboys. They even shared sleeping arrangements and blankets with white cowboys.

Prejudices, opinions formed without knowing the facts, still existed, however. African American cowboys were often hired to do the hardest work, and very few became trail bosses. Yet many earned the respect of their fellow cowboys. A few African American cowboys, such as Bill Pickett, Nat Love, and George McJunkin, earned a place in history.

Back at the Ranch

Finally, after months on the trail, the cattle drive ended. The trail boss sold the cattle. The cowboys, pay in hand, headed for town. They bought new clothes and celebrated. For the first time in months, they sat down to a meal at a real table and bathed in hot water in a bathtub.

Many frontier towns treated African American cowboys the same as other cowboys in the 1870s and 1880s. But **segregation** and prejudice were still widespread. When African American cowboys were treated differently, such as being asked to eat in a separate area, their white trail buddies frequently stood up for them.

After a while (often when their money ran out), cowboys saddled up and headed back to the ranch. In the fall and winter, they watched over the herd and repaired saddles and other equipment to prepare for the spring roundup.

On ranches, cowboys competed with one another
in roping and riding contests.

To pass the time, cowboys matched their
skills in contests. Who could rope a calf
fastest or ride a wild horse longest? Soon
these informal competitions became public
performances, offering prize money. Cowboys
called their new sport a **rodeo** ("a going
around" in Spanish). The tradition of rodeo
competition continues today.

The Cowboy Tradition Lives On

When the West was still mostly unsettled, cattle roamed free. Yet as frontier towns grew, the open range closed. Cattle ranchers fenced their land with barbed wire, which was invented in 1874. After fences were put up, the ranchers needed fewer cowboys to tend their herds.

Meanwhile, more railroad lines cut through the plains. By the 1890s, long cattle drives to the nearest train depot became unnecessary. Some cowboys then worked at big cattle ranches. Others drifted into new jobs.

By the late 1800s, rodeos had become very popular. Also, Wild West shows, which were part rodeo, part circus, and part stage play, had captured the public's attention.

Audiences were charmed by cowboys and stories of their heroic deeds. Some of the most talented cowboys performed in the Wild West shows.

Bill Pickett was a famous African American rodeo star who invented "**bulldogging**." He could "bulldog" a running steer—catch it, ride it, and bring it to the ground—faster than any other cowboy alive. Pickett was in several movies, but never achieved the fame of two of his assistants—Tom Mix and Will Rogers. He became the first African American to be honored in the National Cowboy Hall of Fame.

This movie poster advertised the amazing feats of Bill Pickett.

Another famous African American cowboy was Nat Love. Although not in the movies, he won many riding, roping, and shooting contests. He also told—and no doubt exaggerated—his life story. In his autobiography, printed in 1907, Love claimed to be the role model for the main character in a series of popular cowboy novels of the day.

Nat Love

Like most cowboy stories, Nat Love's autobiography stretches the truth. He tells of fantastic adventures and surprisingly courageous feats. Yet his book is also an important piece of history—reminding us of the important role African American cowboys played in the story of the Old West and in the growth of a young nation.